RAIN FOREST ALERT!

David Bauer

Contents

Rigby®

A Harcourt Achieve Imprint

www.Rigby.com
1-800-531-5015

CHAPTER ONE
Day Interrupted

The day is warm and peaceful in the tropical rain forest.

Tall trees reach upward from the forest roof, their leaves absorbing the sun's energy. Farther down, colorful flowers soak up the sun's warmth, and vines twist around tree trunks. Plants grow everywhere, from many feet above the ground all the way down to the forest floor. Even though little sunlight shines through the **foliage** to the ground, mosses and other plants still live in these shadows. They don't need much sunlight.

This deep, thick forest is the perfect place for many animals to make their homes, too. Insects crawl along the ground, monkeys call to each other among the tree limbs, and birds dart between the leaves. A jaguar naps on a large branch, while a capybara takes a drink from the river.

A steady rain begins to fall, but the animals barely notice. After all, they live in one of the rainiest places on Earth. They enjoy the rain, for it keeps their **habitat** healthy and alive.

Night Monkey

Jaguar

Capybara

3

Suddenly, a loud rumbling noise fills the air. The animals lift their heads in alarm. The jaguar rushes from its tree, and the capybara dives under a bush for protection. The birds scatter, and the monkeys jump away. The noise grows louder and louder. Something is coming nearer, smashing through the trees.

The air is still for a moment. Then a great crash echoes through the forest. The ground trembles, and the leaves shake. A bulldozer comes into view, knocking down trees and clearing the land. People with large saws come through, too, cutting up the trunks and branches into smaller chunks. Soon, large trucks will come to haul the pieces away. Trees and plants and animal homes are wrecked, but the bulldozers and trucks and saws don't stop. The people believe they are making the trees and land more useful for everyone.

But is this really the case?

Loggers use saws to cut trees in the rain forest.

 CHAPTER TWO

What Is a Rain Forest?

Harming any natural habitat can cause serious problems but harming a rain forest is especially troubling. In order to understand why this is so, we should first explore what makes a rain forest so special.

A rain forest is an **ecosystem** filled with plant and animal life. An ecosystem is a group of plants and animals that depend on each other and on their environment in order to live. Scientists think that more than half of the different kinds of the world's plants and animals live in rain forests. That's amazing, considering that rain forests only cover about six percent of Earth's land surface.

70% of the world's species live in rainforests

30% of the world's species live in all other habitats

Equator

N
W—E
S

Map Key
Existing Rain Forest

The main difference between a rain forest and other habitats is the amount of rain the rain forest receives. Rain forests are the rainiest places on Earth. The amount of rain, combined with the warmth, allows for all the different plants and animals you will find in a rain forest.

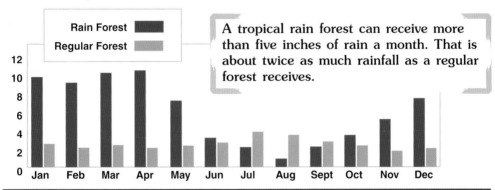

Legend:
- Rain Forest ■
- Regular Forest ■

Values along vertical axis: 12, 10, 8, 6, 4, 2, 0

Horizontal axis: Jan, Feb, Mar, Apr, May, Jun, Jul, Aug, Sept, Oct, Nov, Dec

A tropical rain forest can receive more than five inches of rain a month. That is about twice as much rainfall as a regular forest receives.

Tropical Rain Forest

Temperate Rain Forest

Tropical or Temperate?

Our planet actually has two types of rain forests—*tropical* rain forests and *temperate* rain forests. Tropical rain forests are found near the equator. Average temperatures there are quite warm. Temperate rain forests are found in cooler places between the equater and the poles. They receive less rain than tropical rain forests.

CHAPTER THREE

The Amazon Rain Forest

The largest area of tropical rain forest is in South America. It is the Amazon rain forest, an area of about 1.5 million square miles. That's about half the size of the United States. The area is so large and the land is so varied that thousands of plant and animal **species** live there. A species is what scientists call a single kind of plant or animal. In fact, about one third of all the world's species live in the Amazon rain forest.

A rain forest is made up of four different layers. From top to bottom, these layers are called the **emergent layer**, the **canopy**, the **understory**, and the forest floor.

Imagine yourself flying above the rain forest. You would notice a few trees poking up above everything else. These make up the rain forest's emergent layer. High-flying birds like eagles live there. Now imagine you are floating down through the trees. Beneath the treetops you enter the canopy, where most animals, including monkeys, snakes, and parrots, live. In the canopy the animals find the fruits and flowers they depend on for food.

Below the canopy, but still above the ground, is the understory. Little sunlight reaches this layer, so bushes and shrubs don't get very tall. It might be hard for you to spot the large animals like jaguars and capybaras hiding there in the shadows. Finally you reach the bottom layer of the rain forest, the forest floor. It is home to millions of rain forest insects. People live on the forest floor, too.

Emergent Layer

Canopy

Understory

Forest Floor

Amazing Amazon Plants

The plants you notice first in the rain forest are the trees. Some trees can grow as tall as 150 feet. Although they grow tall, they don't often grow very wide. To support their size, tall rain forest trees must have very strong roots.

Some trees do all they can to reach sunlight. The strangler fig tree wraps itself around the trunk of another tree and climbs up toward the sun.

Some vines also use trees to help them grow. They wrap themselves around a tree's trunk and hang from branches. Animals use the vines to help them move from tree to tree.

An orchid is a kind of flower that grows in the rain forest. Orchids don't grow in soil, because not enough sunlight would reach them. Instead, orchids grow while hanging from rocks and trees.

Orchids are shaped like little cups. Instead of sucking up the water they need through roots, they collect water in their centers. Some tree-dwelling animals drink from the little pools in the center of orchids.

A Tiny Ecosystem

An orchid is a tiny ecosystem. Very small creatures, such as insects and frogs, can actually live inside the small pools of water in an orchid.

Amazing Amazon Animals

Like rain forest plants, animals in the Amazon rain forest **adapt** to life in this warm, rainy environment. Monkeys live high in the rain forest canopy. As they swing from tree to tree, they grip the branches not only with their hands and feet, but they hold on with their tails as well.

The silent hunter among Amazon animals is the jaguar. Its long, sharp claws give it a firm hold when it climbs in the lower limbs of trees, and the dark spots on its fur help it hide among the leaves.

howler monkey

jaguar

Sloths live in the Amazon rain forest, too. They are not as active or quick-moving as monkeys, but they also live among the tree branches. Their hands and feet have a curved shape, like big hooks. The hook shape helps them climb and move through the trees.

Birds, reptiles, insects, and amphibians also live in the Amazon rain forest. The largest of these groups is the insects. Leaf-cutter ants hurry along the rain forest floor, while colorful butterflies dot the trees. Mosquitoes are also common in the Amazon, and if you look closely, you might spot an insect **camouflaged** as a plant.

leaf insect

three-toed sloth

13

Amazing Amazon People

Plants and animals aren't the only things that live in the Amazon rain forest. People live there, too. Some people have moved to the rain forest and set up towns and villages similar to those found almost anywhere. Other people have lived there all their lives, much like their relatives did hundreds of years ago. These people are native to the Amazon.

The native people of the Amazon get everything they need from the rain forest. They hunt for animals, catch fish in the rivers, and raise rain forest plants for food. They use plants and animal skins for clothing, too. They build their homes from the trees and plants around them.

School in the Amazon?

Many Amazon children do not go to school. Instead, they learn about the rain forest and how to live there. Their parents teach them about the natural world and how to get all they need from the rain forest.

CHAPTER FOUR

Rain Forest Products

Tropical rain forests are not only important to the plants, animals, and people who live there. Rain forests are important to everyone around the world. You might be surprised to find out how important rain forests are to you!

Food

Many of the foods we enjoy today were first found in the rain forest. Do you like the taste of chocolate? It comes from cocoa, which grows in the rain forest. Cashews, nuts many people like to eat, also come from the rain forest. What about bananas? They are another rain forest food. Although people now grow some of these foods in other parts of the world, they were all originally discovered in the rain forest.

Cocoa, bananas, and cashews, all come from the rain forest.

cocoa

cashew

bananas

Wood

Many beautiful types of wood come from the rain forest. Mahogany, a deep, red wood, and teak, a pale, hard wood, both come from rain forest trees. Furniture is often made from these types of wood. Rosewood, balsa, and sandalwood also grow in the rain forest. Look around your home or visit a furniture store. You're likely to find tables, cabinets, and other items made from wood that comes from the rain forest.

Mahogany wood is used to make beautiful furniture.

Medicines and Cures

Some of the most important items we get from the rain forest are medicines. About one-fourth of the medicines we have today originally came from plants found in the rain forest. To discover these medicines, scientists experiment with the plants. They remove plant liquids, then they test the liquids to see which plants might cure certain illnesses.

For hundreds of years, the native people of the rain forest have used certain plants to treat and cure illnesses. Now the rest of the world is discovering these uses.

Natives of the rain forest sometimes burn parts of plants to make medicines

A platform makes it easier for scientists to study leaves and flowers high in the rain forest canopy

Even though scientists have learned quite a bit about certain rain forest plants and their medical uses, they still have much to discover. The rain forest has so many plants that scientists have only studied about one percent of them so far. Scientists wonder if the cures for other serious illnesses might lie undiscovered within the plants of the world's rain forests.

CHAPTER FIVE

The Air We Breathe

Perhaps the most important thing we get from rain forests is the oxygen in the air we breathe. People, animals, and plants all need oxygen to live. More than 20 percent of all the oxygen in the air comes from the rain forests!

Rain forests are packed with trees and other plants. Plants absorb gases from the air, including carbon dioxide. Plants also soak up the sun's energy through their leaves. As they do so, they use the sun's energy to change the carbon dioxide into food. The plants then gives off what is left over, like some

of the oxygen in the carbon dioxide. Plants give off more oxygen than they use up, so there is enough oxygen in the air for people and animals to breathe.

Consider the number of plants in a rain forest. Even though rain forests only cover about 6 percent of Earth's land surface, the rain forests have a lot of trees and plants—more trees and plants than any other places on Earth. All these plants give off oxygen. Rain forests, therefore, are necessary for life on Earth. Without rain forests, people and animals would not have enough oxygen to breathe.

Climate Control

Rain forests also help control **climate**. A climate is the temperature and weather conditions of a place. For example, most deserts have a hot, dry climate. Places closer to the equator often have wet, warm climates. Climates farther from the equator are cooler.

Climate is important for many reasons. Farmers depend on the climates where they live to be just right for raising the food we all need. Climate also affects the temperature of the water in the ocean, and many fish can only live in water that is a certain temperature. But how do rain forests help control climate?

Remember the carbon dioxide that rain forest plants absorb from the air? Carbon dioxide in the air traps some of the sun's energy and helps keep Earth a nice, warm place to live. But if there is too much carbon dioxide, then too much of the sun's energy will be held in, and our climate will get too warm.

Farms are ususally located in places that aren't too hot or too cold.

Fewer plants and animals can survive in colder climates.

People in colder climates might want their weather to be a little warmer, but people in warmer areas might not like the weather to get any hotter. Farmers wouldn't want the climate to become too hot or too dry for their crops and animals. And if the temperature of the water rises too much in the ocean, some of the fish might not be able to live. Many scientists call this change in climate **global warming**.

Trees and plants help control climate by absorbing carbon dioxide so there isn't too much of it in the air. This helps to keep Earth's climate from getting too warm. Because Earth's rain forests contain so many trees and plants, they play a very big part in preserving Earth's breathable air and climates.

CHAPTER SIX
A World Without Rain Forests

Think about everything we get from rain forests. They are habitats for thousands of species of animals. They provide food for people to eat and wood for building. They provide homes to thousands of people. Many medicines come from rain forest plants. Perhaps most important of all, rain forests provide our world with oxygen, help control the world's climates, and help keep the air we breathe clean.

Now think about what might happen if the rain forests were all lost. Would this cause problems for our planet?

What would the world be like if the rain forests disappeared? What would our world be missing? How would our world be different, and how would our lives be different?

When you think about it, destroying the world's rain forests does not make sense. Even so, people cut down rain forests every day for many reasons. They believe there is little harm in taking trees from the rain forest and clearing the land.

CHAPTER SEVEN

Why Cut Down the Rain Forest?

Many people think of a rain forest as land that isn't being used. They think that it is better to cut down the rain forest and clear the land to make it useful. People cut down rain forests for several reasons.

Logging

Logging, or cutting down trees for wood, occurs in the rain forest so that people can make things like homes, buildings, furniture, and paper. Some trees are used as fuel, too. Logging companies say that they don't take too many trees and that they always leave plenty of trees behind. But logging has a much bigger effect on rain forests than just the loss of a few trees.

Like many ecosystems, the rain forest is very easily harmed. Plants and animals live everywhere in the rain forest, including on the ground. When a tree falls, not only are the plants and animals living in that tree affected, but the ground is affected as well. As the tree crashes through the forest, it hurts other plants and animals in its path. The tree then pounds the ground, harming any animals or plants that might live there. The heavy machinery needed to haul away the trees and the roads needed for the machinery to travel on hurt the ground even more.

The deep cuts and scratches in the ground made by the machinery and the fallen logs also make it easier for the rain to wash away the rain forest's rich soil. Then new plants and trees cannot grow to take the place of the ones that have been cut down.

A small family farm in the rain forest

Agriculture

Another reason for **deforestation** is to make room for farms. Many farmers use the land already cleared by logging. They plant crops and set up homes on the land. Many of these farmers are native to the rain forest and lost their homes when their part of the rain forest was cleared. They must now adapt to their changing world by becoming farmers.

How much rain forest was lost to create this large farm?

Sometimes sections of the rain forest are cleared to make very large farms. Big companies that grow and sell coffee or sugar will clear the land for their crops. Unfortunately, the soil of the rain forest is not rich enough to support the raising and harvesting of these crops year after year. After a few seasons, the plants can no longer grow, and another area of land must be found and cleared.

Cattle grazing on cleared rain forest land

Big companies also clear rain forest land for raising cattle. Beef cattle need a lot of room to live and grow. Although many beef cattle are raised in the United States, companies look for other places where they can raise even more cattle. A rain forest might appear to be a good place because there seems to be so much unused land. By clearing rain forests of trees, beef producers believe they have found the extra room they need.

Dams

People build dams to control the flow of water. People can then use the flow of water as energy to make electricity. This type of power is called **hydroelectricity**. Rain forest land is sometimes cleared around rivers in order to build dams. The purpose of these dams is to provide electricity to growing towns and villages. Although dams may be necessary to make hydroelectricity, building a dam usually harms the forest around it.

A large dam in the Amazon rain forest

CHAPTER EIGHT
An Alarming Rate

The world's rain forests are now disappearing at an alarming rate. Rain forests cover about six percent of Earth's land. However, rain forests used to cover about fourteen percent of the land on Earth. So our planet has already lost more than half of its rain forests. In fact, every second, about one-and-a-half acres of rain forest, or a piece of rain forest almost the size of two football fields, is cut down every second!

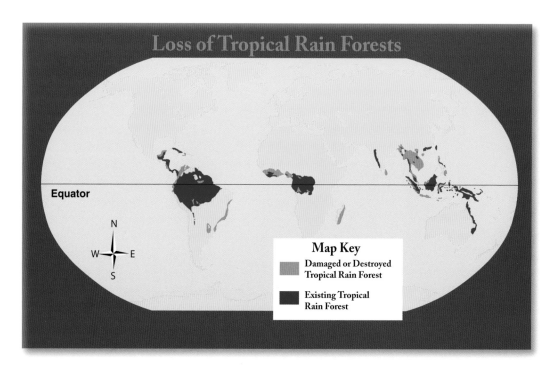

Loss of Tropical Rain Forests

Equator

N
W E
S

Map Key

Damaged or Destroyed
Tropical Rain Forest

Existing Tropical
Rain Forest

At the present rate of deforestation, the Amazon rain forest could disappear in less than 100 years.

Even though people know that the rain forest is important, deforestation continues. Much of the Amazon rain forest covers the nation of Brazil. In 2005, scientists asked the Brazilian government to give them facts about the loss of the Amazon rain forest. The government said that in 2004 alone, more than 10,000 square miles of rain forest were cut down. That's an area a little bit bigger than the state of Maryland! And deforestation in the Amazon has not slowed down.

Rain forests are found in many countries around the world. The bar graph below shows the percentage of the rain forests that each of the countries has lost. The percentages might already seem very high, but what happens if the rain forests continue to be cut down? In a few years, some of these countries might not have any rain forests left at all!

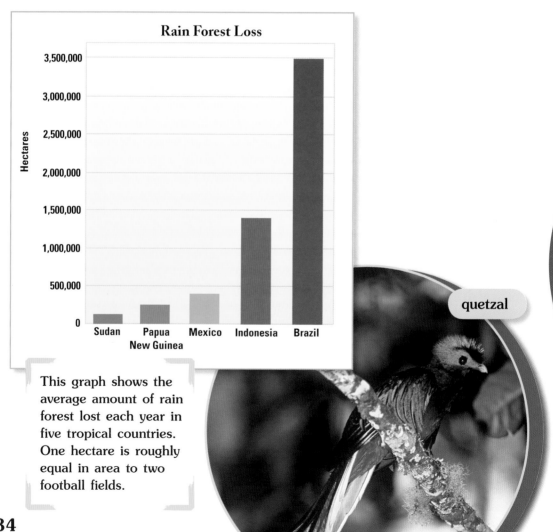

Rain Forest Loss

quetzal

This graph shows the average amount of rain forest lost each year in five tropical countries. One hectare is roughly equal in area to two football fields.

More serious than the loss of land and trees, perhaps, is the loss of plant and animal species. Because so many kinds of plants and animals live in very small areas of the rain forest, harming even a tiny piece means a large loss of life. Scientists guess that every day the planet loses about 137 species of rain forest plants and animals because of deforestation. In a year, that's about 50,000 species that become **extinct**. Scientists fear that important medicines yet to be discovered might also be lost.

golden tamarin

sloth

Melting glaciers could be one result of global warming.

Many scientists believe that the destruction of the rain forests is one of the main causes of global warming. Some of these scientists think that the results of global warming could be really serious. Besides the threat to farming and the temperature of the ocean, scientists say that global warming will make the ice caps at the North Pole and South Pole begin to melt. This would cause the level of the oceans to rise which might lead to flooding in cities near the seashore.

Burning fuels such as coal or oil puts more gases like carbon dioxide into the air. Because of this increase in gases, along with the loss of so many plants and trees due to deforestation, more carbon dioxide is staying in the air. Most scientists believe that the continued loss of the rain forests will prevent us from stopping or slowing down global warming.

CHAPTER NINE

How Can You Help?

One way to help the rain forests is to use less of the things that come from rain forests. For example, if you use less paper, then fewer trees will need to be cut down. Using **recycled** paper also helps.

Talk with your family about buying furniture made from pine or oak wood, which do not come from the rain forest, instead of teak or mahogony wood, which do.

Using waste paper like this to make new paper will save thousands of trees

The best way to help the rain forest, however, is to learn as much as you can about it. Study about the plants and animals of the rain forest. Discover why the rain forest is important to our planet. Learn why people find it necessary to cut down the rain forest, and keep track of deforestation. Find out as much as you can about the effects of global warming.

Once you become informed, you can alert others to the problems of our disappearing rain forests. You can give other people information about the alarming rate of deforestation. You can tell others what our planet will lose if the rain forests are all cut down. This rain forest alert is a problem all over the world. It doesn't only affect the plants, animals, and people that live in the rain forests. It affects us all.

Some effects of deforestation

Glossary

adapt change when necessary

camouflage coloring that allows objects to blend in with their environment

canopy layer of the rain forest that is just below the treetops

climate temperature and weather conditions

deforestation clearing forest land in order to use it for other purposes

ecosystem plants and animals that depend on their environment and on each other to live

emergent layer layer of the rain forest where the tallest trees break through to sunlight

extinct plants and animals that are gone from the earth forever

foliage leaves

global warming the slow heating up of earth's environment

habitat the place where a plant or animal lives

hydroelectricity electricity made with the power of moving water

recycle use a product more than once

species one of a group of plants or animals

understory layer of the rain forest at the level of the lowest branches